Great
DISCOVERIES
& Amazing
ADVENTURES

KINGFISHER
BOSTON

Great DISCOVERIES & Amazing ADVENTURES

CLAIRE LLEWELLYN

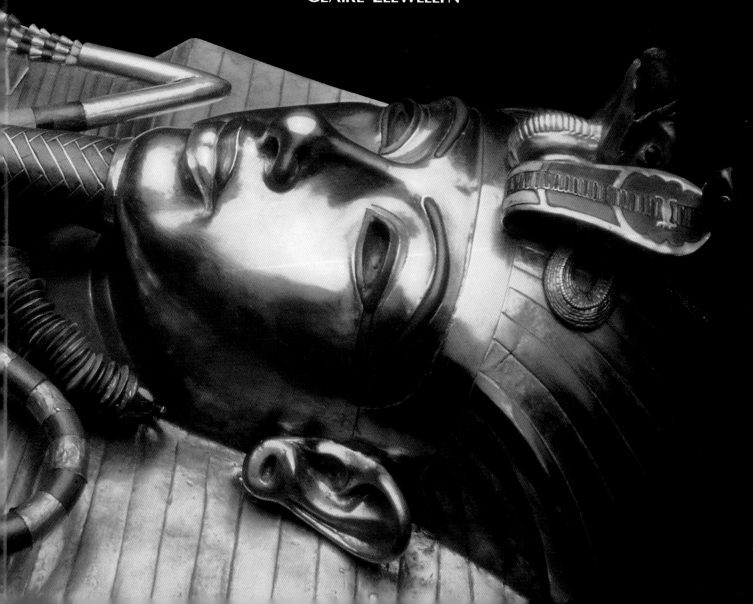

Designed and edited by Bookwork Ltd.

Art editor: Kate Mullins
Art director: Jill Plank
Editorial director: Louise Pritchard

For Kingfisher:

Senior editor: Catherine Brereton
Coordinating editor: Sarah Snavely
Senior designer: Malcolm Parchment
Picture research manager: Cee Weston-Baker
Production controller: Jessamy Oldfield
DTP coordinator: Jonathan Pledge
DTP operator: Primrose Burton
Artwork archivists: Wendy Allison, Jenny Lord

KINGFISHER

a Houghton Mifflin Company imprint
222 Berkeley Street
Boston, Massachusetts 02116
www.houghtonmifflinbooks.com

First published in 2004

2 4 6 8 10 9 7 5 3 1
1TR/0704/SNP/PICA/150MA

LIBRARY OF CONGRESS CATALOGING-IN-PUBLICATION DATA
has been applied for.

ISBN 0-7534-5783-0

Printed in China

CONTENTS

Foreword

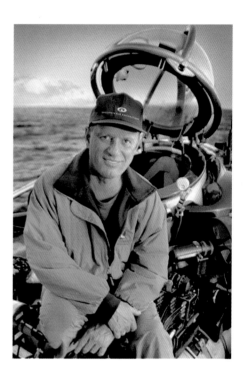

"The deep sea is a great
preserver of human history,
a giant museum waiting for the
next generation of explorers."

I have been very fortunate to participate in a number of great discoveries and amazing adventures in the deep sea. Some involved the exploration of nature's wonders beneath the sea, while others involved discoveries of lost chapters of human history.

My love of adventure in the sea stems from an early childhood interest in Jules Verne's classic novel *20,000 Leagues Under the Sea*, featuring the adventures of Captain Nemo and his crew aboard their mythical submarine the *Nautilus*. As a child watching the movie version of the book, I made an amazing discovery that changed my life forever and helped make me who I am today. The story begins with a battle between the *Nautilus* and a British warship sent to kill what its crew thinks is a huge sea monster. The morning after the warship has been rammed and sunk by the *Nautilus*, a surviving crew member climbs aboard the *Nautilus* and discovers that no one is there. Then he looks out of one of the sub's giant windows to see Captain Nemo and the crew walking on the bottom of the ocean. Walking, I thought! I had thought about swimming, sailing, and surfing, but I had never thought about walking on the bottom of the ocean.

From that day on my view of the ocean changed. I was fascinated with the bottom of the ocean, and when I heard that the greatest mountain ranges on Earth were beneath the sea, I had to see them. In fact, I was one of the first human beings to explore the mid-ocean ridge, the largest mountain range on

Earth. It runs across Earth like the seam on a baseball, stretching for a distance of 43,400 mi. (70,000km). While exploring deep-sea mountain ranges in the mid-1970s we made even greater discoveries—new life-forms that don't live off of the energy of the Sun like plants and animals do but off of the energy of Earth, through a process we now call chemosynthesis. In the rift valley of the mid-ocean ridge we discovered amazing giant tube worms, some five-feet tall with humanlike blood inside their bodies, and swarms of bacteria living inside the worms, carrying out the process of producing food and energy in complete darkness.

That was just the beginning of my discoveries beneath the sea. Only a few years later our team would discover the final resting place of the British luxury liner *RMS Titanic* resting in its watery grave around 11,500 ft. (3,500m) beneath the icy waters of the North Atlantic Ocean. Then we discovered the German battleship *Bismarck* in even deeper water, followed by many other lost ships. Those discoveries led to even more as we looked back farther in time, discovering ancient shipwrecks in the deep sea where no one thought they would be found, some more than 2,700 years old. Now we realize that the deep sea is a great preserver of human history, a giant museum waiting for the next generation of explorers to uncover hundreds of thousands of lost treasures. What is important to remember is that the generation of explorers who are at school right now will explore more of Earth beneath the sea—which covers 72 percent of the globe's surface—than all previous generations combined. This also holds true in outer space and within the human body and mind. So as you enjoy this wonderful book of amazing finds, lost cities, and sunken treasures, pause for a moment and think about the great discoveries and amazing adventures that are awaiting you.

Dr. Robert Ballard

Nature's marvels

Until an unexpected discovery around 180 years ago,
no one knew about the giant reptiles of the past.
The word "dinosaur" had not even been invented.
Earth hides many clues from its millions of years of
history, but sometimes these clues are revealed, and
some amazing finds have been made in deserts,
rocks, marshes, and seas. More and more prehistoric
creatures have been found, ancient creatures
thought to be extinct have turned up alive and well,
and human remains up to 4,000 years old
have been uncovered miraculously preserved.
These major discoveries by curious scientists have
changed our understanding of life on Earth.

Huge reptiles from the past

The *Iguanodon* teeth identified
by Gideon Mantell

For hundreds of years people dug up huge dinosaur fossils without actually understanding what they were. Some people thought they were the bones of dragons; others believed they belonged to giant buffaloes. Then in 1824 an English doctor made a major discovery when he identified the real owner of some huge fossilized teeth.

THE DOCTOR

Gideon Mantell (1790–1852), a doctor in southern England, was a devoted fossil collector. In 1822 he was visiting a patient while his wife waited outside. She noticed some fossils in a pile of stones and picked them up. When she showed them to her husband, he thought they were the teeth of an elephant or another big plant eater.

DETECTIVE WORK

Mantell wanted to find out what the fossils were. He tracked down their original source to a local quarry, where the rocks were around 130 million years old. No large mammals were alive that long ago, so what type of animal could the teeth have belonged to? Mantell continued investigating the unusual fossils.

! DINOSAURS

Mantell's theory that huge reptiles had existed in the distant past began a worldwide fascination with dinosaurs. The word dinosaur, meaning "terrible lizard," was first used by another British scientist, Richard Owen (1804–1892), around 20 years later.

A GIANT LIZARD

Mantell searched through collections of animal skeletons, looking for anything that matched the fossilized teeth. At last he found identical teeth in the much smaller jaw of a modern iguana—a type of lizard. Incredible! Mantell realized that the prehistoric teeth came from a giant lizard, possibly a huge iguana, that was now extinct. He published a description of the teeth and named the animal *Iguanodon*, which means "iguana tooth."

"Now for three months' hard work with my chisel . . ."

DR. GIDEON MANTELL
Fossil collector

Scientists learned more about **Iguanodon** *50 years after Mantell's discovery, when almost 30 complete fossilized skeletons of the animal were found in Belgium. Iguanodon lived in warm forests around 100 million years ago. It measured up to 33 ft. (10m) long and had smooth, scaly skin. It moved around on its hind legs and fed on trees and other plants. It had a sharp, horny spike on its thumb that it used to defend itself against predators.*

Iguanodon with the smaller *Deinonychus*, a fierce predator

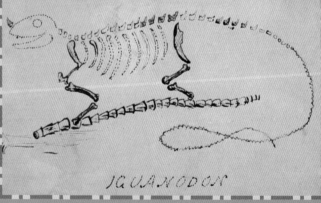

IGUANODON

A drawing by Gideon Mantell of how *Iguanodon* may have looked

THE RECONSTRUCTION

Nine years after Mantell's discovery a large collection of *Iguanodon* bones was discovered in a slab of rock in a quarry in Kent, England. Mantell's friends bought the bones for him for $40. Mantell spent months chiseling the bones apart and drawing examples of how they may have fit together. His ideas proved to be very different from how *Iguanodon* looked. For example, he drew the dinosaur's thumb spike on the end of its nose!

Fossil of an ancient bird

In the mid-1800s scientists were learning more about prehistoric life. They became curious about how ancient creatures related to animals that were alive at the time. Some believed that during Earth's long history animals had changed through a process called evolution. Others believed that they had stayed the same. Then a new fossil was discovered. Scientific understanding was about to take a major step forward.

Archaeopteryx fossil found in 1861, now in the Natural History Museum, London, U.K.

JURASSIC BIRD
The fossil of *Archaeopteryx* was found inside a slab of limestone dating back to the Jurassic period, around 147 million years ago. This makes it the earliest known bird. The skeleton shows the teeth, claws, and long, bony tail of a reptile and the feathers and wishbone of a bird. The fossil is now stored in environmentally controlled conditions in the Natural History Museum in England. It is so fragile and valuable that it is rarely put on public display.

ARCHAEOPTERYX
The discovery of this rare fossil caused a stir in scientific circles and led to a breakthrough in our understanding of evolution. Scientists began examining the links between reptiles and birds and determined that birds evolved from small, meat-eating dinosaurs around 150 million years ago.

REPTILE OR BIRD?
In 1861 a quarryman was working in a limestone quarry in Bavaria, Germany, when he came across an unusual fossil of a birdlike reptile. He gave it to his doctor, Karl Haberlein, to pay off a medical bill. Haberlein collected fossils as a hobby. He realized that the fossil was special and showed it to a geology professor. The professor shocked the scientific world by declaring that this was the fossil of a primitive bird. He named it *Archaeopteryx* from the Greek word for "ancient wing."

SCIENTIFIC DEBATE
One year later Dr. Haberlein needed money for his daughter's wedding. He sold the *Archaeopteryx* fossil to the Natural History Museum in England for around $700, a huge amount of money at the time. The fossil arrived at a controversial time. English scientist Charles Darwin (1809–1882) had just published his book *On the Origin of Species*, in which he expressed his belief that to survive in a changing world, animal species either died out or evolved. Many scientists opposed this theory. Known as procreationists, they supported Christianity's teachings that all animal species were created by God. *Archaeopteryx* became a major part of the debate.

This is how scientists believe *Archaeopteryx* might have looked when it was alive.

Archaeopteryx was around the size of a crow. It had well-developed feathers, teeth, and three long toes with claws. It had clawed fingers on its wings that might have been used to grasp prey.

AN EXCITING NEW THEORY

The procreationists said that *Archaeopteryx* was simply an ancient, long-tailed bird. Darwin's supporters said it was more. In 1868 English scientist Thomas Huxley (1825–1895) argued that birds and reptiles shared so many features that they must be related. The fossil of *Archaeopteryx* was the proof. With its reptile teeth and bird feathers, it was a species in the process of evolutionary change. Recent discoveries support this idea. Fossils from around 123 million years ago have been found in China. With dinosaurlike skeletons and bird feathers, these "dino birds" are similar to *Archaeopteryx*.

An Iron Age human sacrifice

Human remains decay quickly after death, so it is unlikely that a person's body would survive in the ground for 2,000 years. Yet this is what happened in one remarkable case in Denmark. In 1950 the perfectly preserved, 2,000-year-old body of a man was discovered in a peat marsh in Tollund Fen. He became known as Tollund Man. But who was he, and how did he die?

DISCOVERING THE BODY

When two Danish peat harvesters uncovered the face of a man in a peat marsh, they figured he was a recent murder victim and notified the police. Knowing that ancient remains sometimes turned up in the marsh, the police brought experts to the scene. They discovered that the man was around 2,000 years old. They dug him up, packed him in a crate, and sent him to the National Museum in Copenhagen.

Tollund Man's *peaceful expression contradicts his violent death—he was hung by the rope around his neck. He lived during the Iron Age, a period around A.D. 800 in Europe when iron was the main metal used for weapons and tools.*

The remains of Tollund Man in the Silkeborg Museum, Denmark

HOW WAS HE PRESERVED?

Tollund Man was so well preserved because he was buried in a marsh. Organic remains, such as hair, skin, leather, and wood, usually decay in the soil because of bacteria. Bacteria need oxygen to survive, and in a marsh layers of moss prevent oxygen from reaching the lower layers. Also bog water contains acid. This tans skin like leather, preserving it and turning it brown.

*The body was found in **Tollund Fen**. In ancient times the area was home to a group of hunters, whose tools, treasures, and corpses are sometimes found preserved in the marsh.*

TOLLUND MAN

Tollund Man has provided historians with some fascinating remains that have proven to be a huge source of information. He also mesmerizes the wider world. The body of this Iron Age man allows us to find out what life was like in times that were very different from today.

The curled up body of Tollund Man as he was found in Tollund Fen

ASLEEP IN THE PEAT

Tollund Man was found 6.6 ft. (2m) below the surface of the marsh on his side with his arms and legs bent. He was naked except for a hide (animal skin) belt around his waist and a hat on his head. The hat, made out of eight pieces of leather, was laced up under his chin. A braided leather rope was around his neck. This was almost 6.6 ft. (2m) long and formed a noose that could be tightened behind his neck. Tollund Man had short hair and was clean shaven except for some stubble on his lip, cheeks, and chin.

Tollund Man is considered to have the best-preserved head of any early man. Scientists preserved it by soaking it in tubs containing formalin, acetic acid, alcohol, wax, paraffin, and other preservatives.

THE SCIENTIFIC INVESTIGATION

Experts at the museum examined Tollund Man inside and out. From his teeth they estimated that he was more than 20 years old when he died and that he had been hung, probably by the noose around his neck. They examined food remains in his stomach, which showed that his last meal had consisted of a soup of grains and seeds. Grains and seeds are planted in the ground to produce the next season's crop and are a symbol of fertility and growth.

Tollund Man's death after eating this soup may have been a midwinter ritual to ensure the return of the spring.

Ancient body in the ice

It was September 1991. Two hikers were walking in the Ötztal region of the Italian Alps. As they crossed a glacier, they noticed something dark in the ice up ahead. They went to take a closer look and discovered a human body sticking out of the glacier. Whose body was it, and how did it get there in the first place?

ÖTZI'S CLOTHING

From the scraps of leather and dried grass on Ötzi's remains, scientists could see that he was dressed warmly for life in the mountains. He wore a leather loincloth, fur leggings, a coat made out of animal skins, a woven grass cape, and a bearskin hat tied under his chin. His leather shoes had braided grass straps and were filled with grass for warmth.

Ötzi was carrying an unfinished bow around 6.6 ft. (2m) long and arrows in a deerskin quiver (case). He carried other items in a leather sack.

EXAMINING THE BODY

When the two hikers found the body in the ice, they assumed it was the remains of a mountain climber. They reported it to the police, and a helicopter was sent to retrieve the body. Several items lying on the ground close to it were also collected. When forensic scientists examined the corpse, they realized that it was actually very old. They called in Konrad Spindler (b. 1939), an archaeology professor at the University of Innsbruck in Austria. Astonishing! He said the body was prehistoric—more than 4,000 years old.

> ## "It was clear that we were dealing with a prehistoric find."

KONRAD SPINDLER
Archaeology professor

ANCIENT EVIDENCE

News of the discovery caused a great deal of excitement. A prehistoric man had been found with his original tools—a wooden bow, a flint dagger, a wooden ax with a copper blade, and a pouch containing fire-lighting equipment. The scientists who examined him named him Ötzi after the region in the Alps where he was found. They figured out that he was 5 ft. 2 in. (1.6m) tall and had a brown beard and wavy brown hair. He was around 40 years old when he died.

Ötzi was discovered by hikers in an Alpine glacier. He had been buried and preserved by hundreds of years of snow, but as ice on the surface melted, the body was gradually exposed.

RESEARCH CONTINUES

Since being discovered Ötzi has been examined by more than 100 experts. One scientist who was x-raying him found a flint arrowhead in his shoulder. This suggests that Ötzi died after an accident or a fight. He has been on display in the South Tyrol Museum of Archaeology in Bolzano, Italy, close to the place where the body was discovered. But he has been deteriorating. Experts hope that his move to a special refrigerated "igloo" in the museum in December 2003 will help prevent this.

ÖTZI THE ICEMAN

Ötzi is the oldest human mummy to have been preserved by freezing. His discovery opened a window on life near the end of the Stone Age (around 2000 B.C.), a time in which farming spread and people began settling in organized communities. Ötzi has been a huge tourist attraction. Every year thousands of people visit the museum in Bolzano, Italy, to see the prehistoric man.

A living fossil from the deep

Scientists in the 1930s knew all about the coelacanth (pronounced "see-la-kanth")—a fish that had swum in ancient seas long before the age of the dinosaurs and that had died out around 80 million years ago. So just imagine their amazement when, in 1938, a living specimen of one of these ancient fish was caught by fishermen off the coast of South Africa.

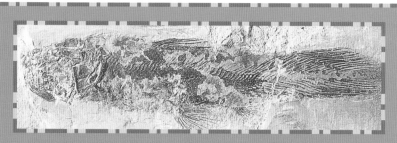

A coelacanth fossil. These fossils date back almost 400 million years.

THE FOSSIL MYSTERY

Scientists learn about ancient creatures by studying the fossils they leave behind. The oldest coelacanth fossils have been found in rocks dating back more than 360 million years, but most of them date from around 240 million years ago, when coelacanth numbers were at their highest. Before the discovery in 1938 coelacanths were believed to have died out around 80 million years ago because more recent fossils were never found. How could the fish disappear for so long and then turn up alive? The answer seems to be that coelacanths changed their habitats from deep to more shallow water inside caves or under reefs close to newly formed volcanic islands. There their remains broke up before they could turn into fossils.

A STRANGE FISH

Marjorie Courtenay-Latimer (b. 1907) was the curator of a tiny museum in the seaport of East London, South Africa. Captain Goosen (d. 1988), a local fisherman, often invited her to inspect his latest catch, and she took interesting specimens for the museum. On December 23, 1938 Courtenay-Latimer was standing on deck when she noticed a blue fin sticking out from a pile of rays and sharks. It was attached to a large fish almost 6.6 ft. (2m) long. No one had any idea what it was, so Marjorie took it with her to find out.

IDENTIFICATION

Courtenay-Latimer searched through her books and found a fish that seemed to match the one she had found. But the fish in her books was prehistoric. She sent a drawing of it to Professor J. L. B. Smith (d. 1968), a fish biologist at a local university. On January 3, 1939 Courtenay-Latimer received a telegram from Smith telling her to preserve the parts that would help him identify it. He hurried to East London. Unbelievable! He identified the fish as a "prehistoric" coelacanth. It was like finding a living dinosaur.

Unlike most fish, whose tails have two sections called lobes, the coelacanth's tail has three lobes. This made the fish very easy for Smith to identify. Coelacanths from east Africa are blue, while Indonesian ones are brown.

A SECOND FISH

A photo of Courtenay-Latimer and her fish was soon in newspapers around the world. Smith longed to find a second coelacanth so that he could study its internal organs. He put up notices all around the east African coast, offering a reward. In December 1952 a fish was caught off the Comoros Islands between Tanzania and the island of Madagascar. Smith was overjoyed. But his fish was more common than he had thought. In 1998 coelacanths were found off Indonesia, 6,215 mi. (10,000km) away.

Marjorie Courtenay-Latimer and her fish

Professor Smith (holding fish) was photographed with the second fish. He later had it preserved.

A living coelacanth in the Indian Ocean off of east Africa

COELACANTH

Marjorie Courtenay-Latimer's discovery of the coelacanth made her famous overnight, and thousands of people came to her museum to see the fish. The species was named Latimeria chalumnae in her honor. It became the zoological find of the 1900s, providing fascinating clues about evolution.

"The most beautiful fish I had ever seen"

MARJORIE COURTENAY-LATIMER
Museum curator

Wild horse of the Asian steppes

Thousands of years ago wild horses roamed Europe and northern and central Asia, grazing on the open grasslands. But around 10,000 years ago the horse population began to dwindle, and at some time in the 1700s they were thought to have become extinct. So it caused a huge sensation when in 1881 Russian explorer Colonel Nikolai Przewalski (1839–1888) discovered herds of wild horses in the grasslands of central Asia.

WILD HORSES

There are many different types of horses. Of all the breeds alive today, including those that live in the wild, only one is not a descendant of the domesticated horse. The odd horse out is the "wild horse of Asia." Its DNA (the genetic code that passes on features to the next generation) is completely different from that of other horses. This wild horse was believed to be extinct.

EXPLORING CENTRAL ASIA

In the late 1800s the ruler of Russia, Czar Alexander II (1818–1881), sent explorers through his vast empire on expeditions of discovery. One of these explorers, Colonel Przewalski (left), made several trips to central Asia. On his way home from an expedition in 1879 he was given the skull and hide of a wild horse by the chief of a border control station. Przewalski was shocked because he had thought that wild horses were extinct. He took the remains to St. Petersburg University, where a zoologist confirmed they were the remains of a wild horse.

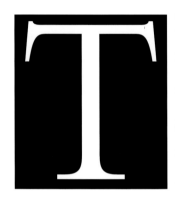

*This **prehistoric painting** of a horse is from the caves in Lascaux, France, (see pages 48–49) and was painted around 17,000 years ago. There are more horses in these paintings than any other animal, suggesting that they existed in huge numbers at that time. They began declining around 10,000 years ago owing to hunting and the loss of their habitat because of a change in Earth's climate.*

PRZEWALSKI'S HORSE

Przewalski's discovery made him famous, and his name lives on in the species he identified, known as Equus przewalskii. *The Russian explorer probably saved the wild horse from extinction. The news of his discovery alerted the world to the plight of the endangered horse. All of the wild horses alive today have descended from 12 that were caught in the wild in around 1900.*

Przewalski's horse is aggressive, fast, and very difficult to tame.

RETURN TO MONGOLIA

Przewalski was determined to find the wild horses. In 1881 he returned to central Asia, and in Mongolia he came across horses grazing near the Gobi desert. They were unlike any horse he had ever seen before. They were small, stocky, and shy. Przewalski had found wild horses. News of the discovery was greeted with amazement and spread across Russia to Europe. In order to save the horse, some foals were captured and taken to Europe to be bred. Today there are around 1,200 of these horses living in captivity; small groups of them are being reintroduced to Mongolia.

Przewalski's horses grazing on grasslands in Mongolia

THE WILD HORSE OF ASIA

Przewalski's horse is smaller than most domestic horses—around 3.9 ft. (1.2m) high to the shoulders and 6.6 ft. (2m) long. It is stocky with a large head and bulging forehead. Like the zebra, it has an upright crest of short, stiff hairs on its head and neck. Its coat varies from dark brown around the mane to pale brown on the flanks and cream colored on the stomach, with a dark stripe along its spine.

Monster on a South Seas island

For years there had been strange rumors about an animal living on Komodo, a remote, rocky island in Indonesia. The creature, which had a reputation as being a fearsome predator, was believed to be a monster from the ancient past. Could these rumors possibly be true? In 1926 an American explorer set out on a long and dangerous journey to Komodo to find out.

The Komodo dragon, the largest lizard in the world

ALL ABOUT KOMODO DRAGONS

The Komodo dragon belongs to a group of giant lizards called monitors. It has short, powerful legs and long claws. From snout to tail it is around 10 ft. (3m) long and weighs around 300 lbs (136kg). Komodo dragons find food by "tasting" the air with their long, forked tongues. The animals are scavengers as well as hunters. They prey on animals such as water buffalo, wild boar, goats, and deer, which they kill by biting and infecting with their poisonous saliva.

AN AMERICAN ADVENTURER

W. Douglas Burden (1898–1978) was a wealthy American hunter looking for adventure. With funding from the American Museum of Natural History, he organized an expedition to find the mysterious "dragons" of Komodo. He hoped to catch a pair and bring them back to New York City. He set out on the 14,915-mi. (24,000-km) trip with a reptile expert, a big game hunter, and his young wife.

> "He swung his grim head this way and that . . . a primeval monster in a primeval setting."
>
> W. DOUGLAS BURDEN
> *Adventurer*

ON TRACK

Not long after their arrival on the island Burden noticed some gigantic footprints—just like fossilized dinosaur tracks he had seen in museums in the U.S. He soon saw the animal that had made them. It was a huge lizard with a gigantic head and forked tongue. Extraordinary! Burden had found the "monster"!

Burden's expedition inspired the movie King Kong *(1933), in which a giant creature is taken to New York City.*

SUCCESS!

Burden returned to New York City with two live Komodo dragons and 12 preserved ones. The live animals were taken to a zoo, and the preserved ones were given to the American Museum of Natural History. Komodo dragons still live on Komodo and a few other islands in Indonesia, but sadly their forest habitat is shrinking because trees are being cut down for timber and to clear land for roads and farms. With only around 5,000 of these creatures alive today, they face an uncertain future.

KOMODO DRAGON

Reports of a living species of giant lizards had come as a complete surprise to experts. When Burden brought back Komodo dragons to New York City, this proved the existence of the remarkable animals and captured the imagination of the public. The expedition was also a personal triumph for Burden.

A Komodo dragon *can burst out of a hiding place at an incredible speed.*

Earth's riches

Throughout history there have been some remarkable discoveries that have revealed Earth's hidden treasures. Explorers, scientists, cowboys, and even an empress have all found amazing things—some by chance, others through dedicated investigations. From simple coffee beans to glittering gemstones, these discoveries have changed the course of people's lives and have even shaped the history of nations.

Riches in a California river

In 1848 a wealthy land developer named John Sutter (1803–1880) was building houses in northern California. He needed a steady supply of timber and decided to build a sawmill in the Sacramento hills. While the mill was under construction the site foreman, James Marshall (1810–1885), noticed some yellow metal glittering in a ditch. Could it be gold?

THE DISCOVERY

John Sutter was building his sawmill in Coloma, a small town on the banks of the American river. Every night the river was redirected to run underneath the mill to form a deep ditch. Every morning the flow was stopped so that the construction work could continue. On January 24, 1848 Sutter's site foreman and partner, James Marshall, noticed some small shiny lumps of metal in the drained ditch. He decided to test one to see if it was gold by smashing it between two rocks. The nugget flattened but did not shatter. Eureka! It was gold.

Miners in California *searched for gold by panning. They scooped gravel into shallow pans and then washed it out. Gold nuggets stayed in the pan because they were heavier than the gravel.*

Gold *is a precious metal with a beautiful color and glow. It is soft and easy to work with and does not tarnish. For thousands of years it has been used to make jewelry and other precious items. Shown here are a gold hair ornament with inlaid diamonds, dating from around 1860 (left), and a lump of pure gold called a nugget (below).*

SUTTER'S SECRET

Marshall showed Sutter the metal. The two men inspected the ditch the next few mornings and found more gold. They figured that the hills must be full of it. Sutter asked his workers to keep the gold a secret until they had finished building the sawmill. But the lure of wealth was too much to control, and his workers left him to look for gold. Soon there was no one left to work at Sutter's mill or for his business.

> # "They got gold fever like everyone else."
>
> JOHN SUTTER
> *Land developer*

FROM RICHES TO RUIN

For Sutter, things got worse and worse. The secret of the gold leaked out, and people flocked to the area. They helped themselves to Sutter's land, and he couldn't do anything about it. Then the Gold Rush began in a frenzy. Tens of thousands of people headed to California to look for gold. Some people made fortunes overnight. Others made nothing at all. Marshall was awarded a small retirement fund in recognition of his discovery, but both he and Sutter died poor, bitter men. The search for gold lasted almost 20 years until the metal became too difficult to find. Today tourists can visit a replica of Sutter's Mill in Coloma and see the spot where Marshall first noticed the gold in a ditch.

THE GOLD RUSH

The Gold Rush began one of the largest human migrations in history. Five hundred thousand people from around the world endured long, dangerous journeys by land and sea to reach California. Arriving in 1849 the "forty-niners," as the new immigrants were called, discovered a harsh reality. Life in the gold fields was lonely and dangerous, and mining was backbreaking work. Many of them found nothing, and those who made money often drank or gambled it away. Some miners became merchants and earned a fortune selling goods and services for hugely inflated prices.

A replica of Sutter's Mill, part of the Marshall Gold Discovery State Historic Park in Coloma, California

A secret world underground

In 1901 a 19-year-old cowboy named Jim White was working near the town of Carlsbad in the mountains of New Mexico. One evening he saw a strange black cloud emerging from the ground. It turned out to be millions of bats flying out of a hole. Where could they be coming from? White decided to explore.

*In the summer Carlsbad Caverns is home to seven species of bats, including the **Mexican freetail bat** (right). During the day around five million bats sleep in the caverns. In the evening they all stream out.*

THE BATS' HOME

Jim White returned to the hole in the ground with a lantern and some rope and wire. He built a simple ladder and climbed down into the hole. He soon found himself 148 ft. (45m) underground, standing in piles of bats' droppings. He climbed through an opening in the rock. Jackpot! White had entered an enormous cavern with huge stalagmites rising from the floor and stalactites hanging from the ceiling. It was a breathtaking sight.

THE GUANO MINE

White returned to explore the caverns many times. He found passageways and chambers, some large enough to contain a cathedral. He told people about his discovery, but no one believed him. Then a merchant from Carlsbad bought the mining rights to the cavern—the bat droppings, called guano, would make valuable fertilizer. He drilled a shaft into a cavern and rigged a steel bucket to collect the guano.

HOW THE CAVERNS WERE FORMED

The Carlsbad Caverns National Park contains around 100 caverns with high, vaulted ceilings and amazing rock formations. Geologists believe that the limestone caverns first formed more than 200 million years ago when an undersea reef was raised above sea level and was then hollowed out by seeping groundwater. When the groundwater was gone, the hollows in the rocks filled up with air. Finally, over thousands of years, dripping rainwater deposited minerals, which built the formations that can be seen today.

On summer evenings visitors wait to watch swarms of bats leaving the caverns to feed.

A NATIONAL MONUMENT

White was obsessed with the caverns and worked as a miner in them for 20 years. He spent his free time exploring the underground world. Eventually the mine closed down, but White stayed put. One day he persuaded some Carlsbad citizens to go down in the old guano bucket to visit the caverns. A photographer went with them, and his pictures of the wonderful rock formations caused a sensation. News of the caverns soon reached the government in Washington, D.C., and in 1923 government inspectors went to look at the caverns. They reported back, and the site was soon declared a national monument.

*By the light of a lantern, Jim White saw a **huge cavern** containing stalagmites and stalactites.*

CARLSBAD CAVERNS

Jim White's discovery changed his life. He dedicated his lifetime to exploring the caves and sharing their wonders with others. When the Carlsbad Caverns National Park opened, White was the first head ranger. Today the caverns are one of the most famous tourist attractions in the U.S. Around 800,000 people visit them every year.

Hot spots on the ocean floor

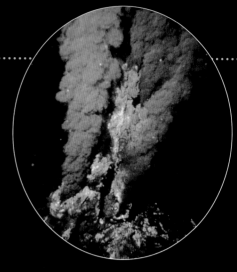

D eep–sea vents are cracks in Earth's crust where hot water gushes up through the seabed. In the 1960s scientists studying the chemistry of the oceans predicted that vents exist, but no one had ever found one. In 1977 explorer Robert Ballard (b. 1942) was determined to find one.

WAITING FOR A SIGN

Onboard a ship near the Galàpagos Islands in the Pacific Ocean Robert Ballard and a team of scientists were searching for signs of a deep-sea vent. They were towing a steel cage called *Angus* along the ocean floor. *Angus* had lights, a camera, and temperature sensors that could detect warm water. One night *Angus* sent out a signal. It had found a hot spot!

*On a later expedition Ballard found vents that are now called **black smokers**. The "smoke" is hot water that looks dark because it is full of dissolved material. This material settles around the vent and builds a chimneylike structure that extends up many yards.*

FINDING A VENT

The next morning three scientists climbed into a submersible called *Alvin* and dived down more than 1.2 mi. (2km) to the hot spot. They saw warm, shimmering water bubbling up through cracks in the seabed. Incredible! They had found a deep-sea vent. The hot water turned cloudy as it mixed with the sea, and material that had been dissolved in it stained the seabed brown.

A spider crab picks its way over small tube worms on the seabed near a deep-sea vent.

LIFE AROUND THE VENTS

The area around deep-sea vents teems with white crabs, huge tube worms, giant clams, shrimps, and many other creatures. For most of the time this undersea community survives in icy darkness, but occasionally it is blasted by boiling water and sometimes destroyed by flows of molten rock. In some places bright red tube worms grow up to 6.6 ft. (2m) long (see main picture, right). They live inside tubes of horny material, which protect them from predators such as crabs.

WHAT CAUSES THE VENTS?

Deep-sea hydrothermal vents are deep cracks in the seabed caused by movements of Earth's crust. Seawater seeps down through the cracks and is heated by molten rock underneath Earth's surface. The hot water later gushes out of the vents, carrying gases and dissolved material from deep inside Earth.

A SURPRISING DISCOVERY

The scientists in *Alvin* made another discovery that came as a complete surprise—there were hundreds of clams and other animals living around the vents. Finding life in this dark place where water gushed out at fiery temperatures was extraordinary. What could the animals be feeding on? It turned out to be bacteria, which were feeding on the gases and materials pouring out of the vents. Up until this discovery it was a common belief that all energy for life came from the Sun. But the energy for this life was coming from deep inside Earth.

Scientists watched the amazing community of animals from the submersible Alvin. *This high-tech mini submarine is 23 ft. (7m) long and can carry a pilot and two scientists down 14,760 ft. (4,500m). It has lights, cameras, and robotic arms that collect samples.*

DEEP-SEA VENTS

The discovery of deep-sea vents was one of the most important oceanographic discoveries of the 1900s. It proved that some animals were supported by energy from underneath Earth's surface. This changed our view of life and helped explain the chemistry of the oceans.

Fuel for a new age

People always knew that oil existed in Texas. For hundreds of years it had been seeping out of the ground, but no one tried to drill for it until the late 1800s. The first oil wells produced so little that they were shut down. But one geologist was convinced that there was more oil, and he was determined to find it!

THE SEARCH FOR OIL

American geologist Patillo Higgins (1863–1955) believed that there was oil under a small hill known as Spindletop near the town of Beaumont, Texas. Locals thought Higgins' ideas were nonsense, but he hired an engineer named Anthony Lucas (1855–1921) to begin drilling in the area. After awhile Higgins ran out of money, and he pulled out of the enterprise. But Lucas wanted to keep trying, so he formed a new company with a team of oil workers. They surveyed the area, chose a spot, and began drilling in October 1900. By Christmas they had found nothing and stopped for the holidays.

*On the morning of January 10, 1901 oil gushed out of a hole in the ground on a hill called Spindletop near Beaumont, Texas. The greenish-black **oil gusher** measured around 6 in. (15cm) across and rose to a height of more than 165 ft. (50m), doubling the size of the drilling derrick (right). This was more oil than had ever been seen anywhere else in the world.*

OIL IN SPINDLETOP
The discovery of oil reserves in Spindletop opened people's minds to the potential of the fuel. New machines like cars and planes were invented, sparking an industrial revolution in the U.S. and leading to an economic boom.

A crew stands by to repair an oil well in Beaumont, Texas

THE OIL BOOM

Following the discovery of oil the population of Beaumont grew from 10,000 to 50,000 practically overnight. Production went wild, with close to 300 wells fighting for space on top of Spindletop. Swindlers moved in, persuading people to invest in hoax oil companies that never made any money. Soon Spindletop became known as "Swindletop."

THE GUSHER

Work began again in the new year, and the drillers quickly reached a depth of 985 ft. (300m). Then on the morning of January 10, 1901 something remarkable happened. As drillers lowered the drill into the hole, mud bubbled up to the surface, and the drill shot out of the ground. A short silence followed, and then with a noise like a cannon shot, something black gushed out of the hole. It was oil!

THE OIL AGE

Lucas had hoped to find a well that would produce five barrels of oil per day (one barrel is equal to 42 gal./159L). The Spindletop well produced almost 100,000 barrels per day—more than all of the other oil wells in the U.S. combined! Oil is still a big business in Texas. It is the second-largest oil-producing state in the U.S. after Alaska and provides the raw materials for the huge petrochemical industry in Houston.

The discovery of huge reserves of oil led to the invention of the car, fueling America's manufacturing industry.

A fortune in the ground

In 1866 Hopetown was just a tiny village in the British Cape Colony in southern Africa. One day a young Hopetown farmer, Schalk van Niekerk (c. 1824–1880), was visiting a neighbor when he saw the neighbor's teenage son playing with a shiny white pebble. Van Niekerk was interested in unusual stones, and something about this pebble caught his eye. He convinced his neighbors to let him take the pebble home to find out more about it.

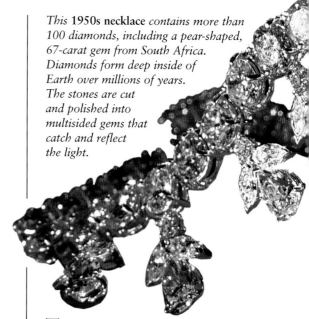

This 1950s necklace contains more than 100 diamonds, including a pear-shaped, 67-carat gem from South Africa. Diamonds form deep inside of Earth over millions of years. The stones are cut and polished into multisided gems that catch and reflect the light.

THE GLIMMERING PEBBLE

Van Niekerk showed the stone to a merchant, who sent it to an expert. Astonishing! It was a 21-carat diamond (one carat is 0.007 oz.). It was bought by the Governor of the Cape Colony for $800. It was known as the "Eureka" because it was the first diamond found in South Africa.

DIAMOND RUSH

Hopetown boomed in the diamond rush. Miners bought claims to small plots of land, set up camp, and began digging. Later, when miners moved to Kimberley, Hopetown became an important supply town, and farmers were paid huge prices to deliver goods north. Wild spending sprees took place in the town—men lit cigars with money, and women bathed in champagne! But the boom and the excitement did not last—when a new railroad bypassed Hopetown on its way to the Kimberley mine, the town was quickly forgotten.

Diamond mining was dangerous work, and European settlers' greed for diamonds drove them to abuse African workers.

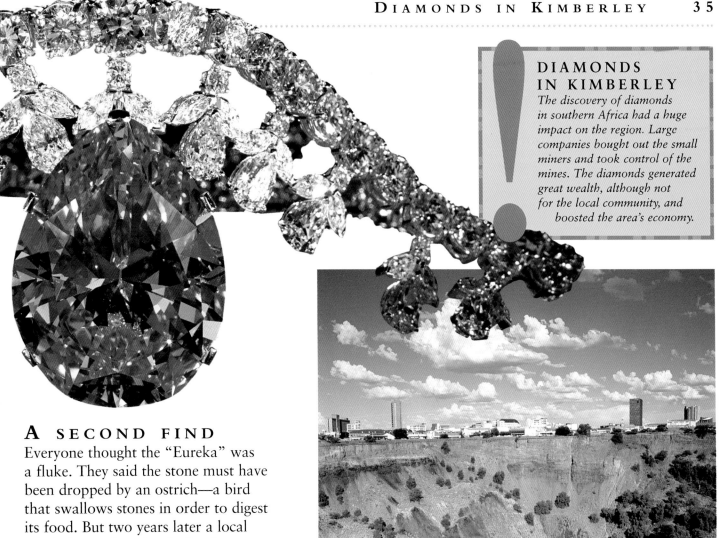

The Kimberley mine became known as the "**Big Hole**" and now forms part of an open-air museum. The "Eureka" diamond is also on display at the museum.

A SECOND FIND

Everyone thought the "Eureka" was a fluke. They said the stone must have been dropped by an ostrich—a bird that swallows stones in order to digest its food. But two years later a local witch doctor found a similar, larger stone in the same area. He took it to Schalk van Niekerk, who exchanged it for 500 sheep, ten oxen, and one horse. The stone turned out to be an 83-carat diamond, later named the "Star of South Africa."

> ## "This is the rock on which the future success of South Africa will be built."

RICHARD SOUTHEY
Colonial Secretary of the Cape (1834–1899)

DIAMOND FEVER

Tens of thousands of treasure seekers rushed to Hopetown in the Northern Cape in the hope of finding their own diamonds. The Diamond Rush had begun! The miners moved from place to place, following each new find. They settled around 60 mi. (100km) north of Hopetown in an area that became known as Kimberley. This was the start of southern Africa's diamond industry, and today this region is still one of the biggest diamond producers in the world.

The mighty secret of Africa

Around 150 years ago a large part of Africa had not been explored by Europeans. Geographers longed to discover its secrets, especially the source of the Nile river. In 1856 the Royal Geographical Society in London, England, sent an expedition to find it.

THE EXPEDITION

Richard Burton (1821–1890) and John Hanning Speke (1827–1864) led the expedition. They arrived on Africa's eastern coast in June 1857 and headed west through what is now Tanzania. Five months and 600 mi. (960km) later they reached Tabora. There they were told about a huge lake to the west, and they went to explore it. They found the lake (Lake Tanganyika)—but no river flowing north. By now it was May 1858, and their health was suffering. They returned to Tabora to rest.

The Nile river is the longest river in the world. It flows north out of Lake Victoria in Uganda to the Mediterranean Sea. The Ripon Falls, which Speke identified as the river's source, became submerged in 1954 after the Owen Falls dam was built.

SOURCE OF THE NILE

John Hanning Speke's discovery of the main source of the Nile solved one of the mysteries of 19th-century geography. But Speke was not consistent in his methods, and he could not provide solid proof about the source of the Nile. It was not until 1875 that the explorer and journalist Henry Morton Stanley (1841–1904) proved beyond a doubt that Speke was right.

Author, explorer, scientist, and poet, Richard Burton was a remarkable man with a fiery temper. He was a very talented linguist and spoke more than 30 languages. He loved Arab culture and often wore eastern clothes—such as this **hat** *and* **shoes**.

Burton's flat-topped Muslim hat, known as a fez

Eastern slippers with curled toes worn by Burton

John Hanning Speke *was a former soldier in the Indian army. After ten years' of service he planned to explore Africa to gather specimens of rare birds and other animals. Instead he joined Burton's expedition. A serious and conservative man, he was the opposite of eccentric Burton.*

SPEKE'S DISCOVERY

Back in Tabora, the expedition group was told about another huge lake to the north. Unfortunately Burton was too sick to move, so Speke set out to investigate on his own. In August 1858 he found and named the enormous Lake Victoria, which he was convinced was the source of the Nile. Speke returned to Burton with the news of his discovery, but Burton thought that Speke was wrong, and the two men argued. Exhausted, they decided to return to England.

THE SOURCE IS FOUND

Speke arrived in London, England, before Burton and went to the Royal Geographical Society with his findings. By the time Burton arrived, Speke had been commissioned to lead a new expedition to settle the Nile river question once and for all. Speke set out in 1860. In July 1862 he found and named the Ripon Falls to the north of Lake Victoria. He had found the source of the mighty Nile river at last.

END OF A FRIENDSHIP

Burton and Speke were at odds before they returned to England. They had agreed to speak to the newspapers together, but before Burton arrived in England Speke had announced that he thought Lake Victoria was the source of the Nile. After Speke's second expedition Burton still thought he was wrong, and the day before they planned to have a public debate on the issue, Speke died in a shooting accident.

Speke (standing left) presents his case to a meeting of the Royal Geographical Society. Burton is standing on the right.

Coffea arabica, the coffee plant

Berries for a special drink

In the 900s, according to legend, a goatherd named Kaldi was grazing his goats in the Ethiopian mountains. One night he noticed they were behaving in a strange way. Instead of sleeping soundly like they usually did, they were wide awake and jumping around. The goatherd decided to investigate—and discovered something that became popular all over the world.

COFFEE CULTIVATION

Coffee is such a popular drink that it is now cultivated on farms and plantations in more than 50 countries. The plant will grow only in tropical regions, where the weather is always warm. After flowering the berries, known as cherries, form on the plant. These change color as they ripen—from green to yellow and finally to red. Inside each cherry are two green beans that turn brown when they are roasted. These are ground and mixed with hot water to make the drink we call coffee. Each plant produces around 2,000 cherries in a growing season, enough to make 1.2 lbs (500g) of roasted coffee.

Harvesting coffee beans in Costa Rica

FRISKY GOATS

When Kaldi the goatherd took his goats into the mountains, he knew that they would find enough to eat. They could survive in much more difficult conditions. When they did not go to sleep as usual, Kaldi remembered that he had seen them eating berries from some small bushes, and he went to look at the plants. They had glossy leaves, white flowers, and hard berries the same size and color of cherries. Kaldi tasted the berries and began feeling lively and more awake. Amazing! He had discovered the effect of coffee.

STRANGE BREW

Soon after a Muslim monk passed by, and Kaldi told him about the berries he had found. The monk picked some and took them to his monastery. There he crushed them and mixed them with hot water. He found that when he drank some of the bitter-tasting brew, it helped him stay awake during long hours of prayer. He and his fellow monks began supplying other monasteries with the "Kaffa" berries, named after the region in Ethiopia where they were found. The "Kaffa" drink quickly became very popular.

The world's first **coffee shop** *opened in 1475 in Constantinople, Turkey. Coffee quickly became so popular that it was banned by the ruling sultan. The ban had little effect, and coffee drinking boomed.*

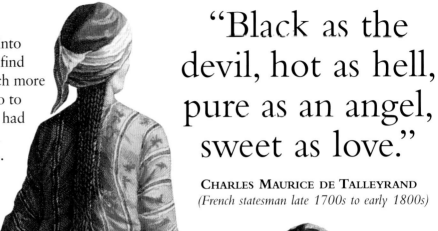

"Black as the devil, hot as hell, pure as an angel, sweet as love."

CHARLES MAURICE DE TALLEYRAND
(French statesman late 1700s to early 1800s)

An engraving from the 1700s of "a Turkish girl taking coffee on a sofa"

COFFEE

The discovery of coffee brought a completely new drink to the world. Coffee was also used in some countries as a medicine. The impact of the drink was small at first, but over hundreds of years its popularity spread around the world. Today around 400 billion cups are enjoyed worldwide every year.

COFFEE TRAVELS

Coffee traveled with traders from Africa across the Red Sea to Arabia and then to Turkey. In Turkey people used only the beans inside of the berries. They roasted them, ground them, and boiled them in water. In the early 1600s coffee reached Europe. Pope Clement VIII (pope 1592–1605) liked it so much that he baptized it and gave it his approval. Gradually a craze spread throughout Europe and later to the U.S. Cafés sprang up where people could meet and talk about the news of the day. Coffee is still a social drink—and a global industry.

Luxury in ancient China

Around 4,700 years ago Emperor Huang-Ti of China (c. 2704–2598 B.C.) had a beautiful garden. He was very proud of it but was worried because something was damaging his mulberry trees. He asked his wife, Hsi-Ling-Shi, to find out what it was. What she found became worth its weight in gold.

Farmed silkworms spinning cocoons

HOW SILK IS MADE

Silk is a delicate cloth woven from silkworm threads. This tiny creature, the caterpillar of the *Bombyx* moth, spins a cocoon from a long, sticky thread before changing into an adult. When several threads are spun together, they form a strong, glossy yarn that can be woven into silk. Today most silk comes from small farms in China and the Far East, where it is a major "green" industry. It does not cause waste or pollution, and its raw materials are renewable resources.

THE EMPEROR'S GARDEN

Hsi-Ling-Shi was only 14 years old when, according to legend, she went to inspect her husband's mulberry trees. She discovered that white caterpillars were eating the leaves and then spinning shiny cocoons around themselves. Hsi-Ling-Shi tried to kill the caterpillars in hot water, but as she put a cocoon in the water, she noticed that it unraveled into a long thread.

WEAVING SILK

The empress was intrigued by the thread. She twisted it into a yarn and then wove it into cloth. The material was smooth and shimmered in the light. Amazing! She had discovered silk. Soon she had her own mulberry trees and looms on which her servants wove the precious cloth. When the silk was dyed, it shone with rich colors and made luxurious gifts for visitors to the emperor's court.

This rare **Chinese silk robe** *dates from the time of the emperor Qianlong (ruled 1736–1795). It is richly embroidered with a pattern of dragons.*

This **terra-cotta camel,** *dating from A.D. 618–907, is carrying silk. Trade flourished along the Silk Road, with traders carrying cloth, spices, and other goods from China to the Mediterranean Sea.*

THE SECRET OF SILK

In time silk was taken to the West along a trade route known as the Silk Road. Its luxury was greatly admired all over the world. For the next 3,000 years the Chinese kept silk production a closely guarded secret. Eventually, in around A.D. 550, Roman emperor Justinian (482–565) sent two spies to China. They smuggled silk moth eggs and mulberry seeds inside their walking canes, and China's great secret was finally revealed.

SILK

The discovery of silk brought great wealth to ancient China. The appetite for silk in the West strengthened trading ties between Rome and China, and the Silk Road, a 2,490-mi. (4,000-km)-long trade route, developed. Traders shared their cultural customs, so ideas were exchanged between East and West.

Lost wonders

Every year thousands of tourists marvel at the
terra-cotta army of a Chinese emperor, the Inca
city of Machu Picchu, and the prehistoric cave
paintings in Lascaux, France. They are famous today,
but many of the world's greatest historical treasures
were shrouded in mystery for hundreds or even
thousands of years. Some were only known by the
local people until explorers stumbled across them or
searched for them and introduced them to the wider
world. Others were hidden completely, buried in the
ground, under the sea, or sealed in secret caves.
Their discovery has helped us uncover a wealth
of information about human history—about the
rise and fall of great civilizations and the lives
of both ordinary people and famous rulers.

A hidden city in the Andes

Between A.D. 1100–1500 the mighty Inca civilization flourished high up in the Andes mountains of Peru in South America. In 1532 Spanish adventurers known as *conquistadores* (conquerors) invaded the region and ransacked many Inca cities in search of gold. The Incas abandoned their other cities, which fell into ruin. One of these cities was Machu Picchu.

THE PROFESSOR

Hiram Bingham (1875–1956), a history professor at Yale University, studied South American history for many years. In 1911, during a visit to Lima, Peru, he came across an old book that told of the downfall of the Incas. He was inspired by the description of the Inca retreat and the ancient mountain cities that they had abandoned. Bingham decided to try to find the ancient Inca capital city.

"I know of no place in the world [which] can compare with it."

HIRAM BINGHAM
History professor

Machu Picchu *stands on a remote ridge in the Andes mountains, around 8,200 ft. (2,500m) above sea level. The town, overlooked by towering peaks, was abandoned by the Incas. Amazingly the Spanish never found it during the 300 years that Peru was part of the Spanish Empire.*

A NERVE-RACKING CLIMB

Bingham led an expedition to Peru. He went with his party to Cuzco in the foothills of the Andes. From there they climbed into the Urubamba gorge. On July 23, 1911 the group camped on the land of a local farmer, who told Bingham about ruins on top of a ridge. Bingham paid the farmer to guide him there, and the two set out one cold, drizzly morning. It was a nerve-racking climb up steep, rocky slopes and along narrow mountain paths. At times the professor had to crawl on his hands and knees across narrow bridges stretching over terrifying gorges.

A SENSATIONAL FIND

At the top of the ridge Bingham and the farmer rested in a hut, where locals told them about the nearby ruins. An 11-year-old boy escorted the professor past overgrown terraces to some white granite walls. Bingham saw palaces, temples, terraces, and towers. Astonishing! It was an ancient Inca city, known to locals as Machu Picchu. Bingham was overwhelmed. He led three additional expeditions to Machu Picchu over the next four years.

Sculpted granite blocks in the Royal Tomb of Machu Picchu beneath the Temple of the Sun

BUILDING MACHU PICCHU

Built in 1450, Machu Picchu, or "old mountain," is a spectacular, highly ordered city covering a site of around 3 sq. mi. (8km²). Its houses, temples, workshops, and other buildings were built using a simple design. Large granite blocks were shaped and sanded by hand until they fit together perfectly without needing mortar. There were no rounded arches or decorative carvings. On the outskirts of the city the steep hillsides were terraced for farming, and fertile soil was brought up from the valley to grow sweet potatoes, sugarcane, yucca, and corn.

A broken palace on the seabed

O n April 14, 1912 the cruise ship *Titanic*, on its maiden voyage, struck an iceberg in the North Atlantic Ocean. It sank, and more than 1,500 passengers died. Over the next 70 years many people tried to locate the wreck, but it was like looking for a needle in a haystack. Then, in September 1985, Robert Ballard (b. 1942) found the *Titanic's* watery grave.

*These **silver objects** from the* Titanic's *dining rooms are some of the 6,000 or more objects that have been recovered from the seabed around the wreck. Other items include china and porcelain, clothing, postcards and letters, newspapers, and the ship's bell. These artifacts have been preserved by a team of experts, and many are now part of a touring exhibition to museums around the world.*

*Many wealthy people were tempted to sail on the **Titanic's** maiden voyage. The ship symbolized style, glamour, and luxury. It was no surprise that manufacturers used the ship's prestige to advertise their products. In this poster a soap company boasts that its luxury soap has been chosen for the first-class passenger cabins.*

LUXURY TO DIE FOR

The *Titanic* was the largest vessel of its time. It was a floating palace that rivaled the best hotels on land. Built using only the finest materials, the ship offered top-notch first-, second-, and third-class cabins. It also contained elegant public rooms, a grand staircase, a Parisian-style café, a Turkish bath, a gymnasium, and squash courts. A one-way ticket in a first-class suite cost around $750— the equivalent of a working person's salary for an entire year.

WHO IS ROBERT BALLARD?

Robert Ballard is an American geologist, marine scientist, and ocean explorer. He has taken part in many expeditions to explore the seabed and its ancient wrecks. He was enthralled by the story of the *Titanic* and was sure that, with the right team and high-tech equipment, he could find the wreck. In 1985 he and a group of American and French scientists began their quest. They planned to search the seabed in the area of the *Titanic's* last reported position and then follow the course where any debris from the ship would have drifted on that fateful night.

FIRST SIGHTING

Ballard and the French
co-leader, Jean-Louis Michel
(b. 1945), searched the ocean
floor. They used the latest
sonar equipment and a
deep-sea video camera
called *Argo*. But all they
saw was mud and sand.
Then, when only five days
of the expedition remained,
pipes, deck parts, and a huge
boiler appeared on the video
screen. Michel grabbed the *Titanic's*
construction records and found
the picture of its boiler. It exactly
matched the boiler on the screen.
They had found the long-lost wreck!

The **wreck of the** *Titanic was discovered
371 mi. (598km) southeast of Newfoundland,
Canada, and 2.5 mi. (4km) beneath the surface of
the ocean. As it sank, the ship broke into two huge
pieces, which now lie 2,000 ft. (610m) apart.*

MOVING PICTURES

Over the next four days *Argo* explored
the wreck more closely. But then the
expedition's time was up, and Ballard
had to leave the site. The wreck's
location was kept a closely guarded
secret. The next summer Ballard
returned to the *Titanic*, diving
down in the submersible *Alvin*.
Using a small robot that could get
inside the wreck, he recorded moving,
eerie pictures of the grand staircase
and other elegant fixtures. Ballard
never forgot that the *Titanic* was a
grave, and when his expedition ended,
he left behind a plaque that reads:
"In memory of those souls who
perished with the *Titanic*
April 14/15, 1912."

Ancient pictures in a hidden cave

I n September 1940 four boys were walking in the grounds of Lascaux, an old mansion in southwest France. When their dog fell through a crack in some rocks, the boys went to rescue it and found that the hole led to a cavern. It would prove to be one of the most exciting archaeological discoveries of the 1900s.

A painting of cattle on the cave walls of Lascaux

CAVE ART

The artists who painted the pictures in Lascaux drew animals that were important to them. They might have thought that the paintings would help them while hunting. It must have been difficult to work in the dark, remote caves. The artists would have needed torches to see and ladders to reach the high ceilings. The paints they used were made from natural pigments, plant roots, charcoal, and sap and were dabbed on using their fingers or with sticks or pads of moss or fur.

The insides of the **Lascaux** *caves are covered with pictures—some are painted, and others are engraved or drawn. The pictures were made around 17,000 years ago during the early Stone Age, when people had not yet discovered metals and were using stone to make tools.*

FINDING THE CAVE

The four teenage boys who discovered the cavern were Marcel Ravidat, Jacques Marsal, Georges Agnel, and Simon Coencas. The next day they returned to explore. They brought ropes, ladders, and lights with them and lowered themselves down through the hole. Their eyes gradually adjusted to the darkness. They saw that the walls of the cavern were covered in pictures. They could see images of horses, deer, and other animals. The boys knew they had made an amazing discovery.

THE CAVES OF LASCAUX

The caves of Lascaux were one of the great archaeological discoveries of the 1900s. The paintings of prehistoric animals captured the world's imagination. They offer us a glimpse of the lives of our ancestors in the distant past.

A group of tourists
visit the replica cave

THE FIRST VISITORS

News of the discovery traveled fast. People were soon flocking to explore the caves. In all, they found seven underground chambers connected by narrow passageways, with paintings and engravings on the ceilings and walls. A team of top archaeologists soon arrived at the caves. They were amazed by the sensational find—the paintings dated from around 15000 B.C. and were perfectly preserved. Archaeologists were worried about what to do with the caves. Europe was involved in World War I, so there was no spare money to spend on developing and protecting the site. They decided to seal the caves until after the war.

VISITS TO THE CAVE

The caves were opened to the public in 1948, and thousands of people visited them. But it soon became clear that the visitors were having a harmful effect. The gases and water vapor in their breath dampened the cave walls and damaged the precious paintings. Attempts were made to protect them, but in 1963 it was decided to close the caves. Twenty years later a life-size replica of the biggest cave was opened nearby.

Secrets of an ancient text

The monuments and tombs of ancient Egypt are inscribed with a form of picture writing known as hieroglyphs. For centuries people puzzled over these mysterious symbols, trying to decipher them. Then in 1799 a stone slab was stumbled upon in the Egyptian desert. It became one of the most famous discoveries from ancient Egypt.

FINDING THE STONE

In the late 1790s French Emperor Napoleon Bonaparte (1769–1821) and the French army invaded Egypt. In 1799 soldiers began digging the foundations of a fort in the town of Rashid (known in English as Rosetta) on the Nile delta. As they dug in the sand, one of them came across a slab of black stone.

LANGUAGES AND SCRIPTS

One side of the stone was covered with an inscription, a decree issued in 196 B.C. by Egyptian priests supporting Ptolemy V (c. 210–180 B.C.), the new Greek-born king of Egypt. The decree itself was not very interesting, but the way it was written was. The same piece of text had been inscribed three times: in Greek, Egyptian hieroglyphs, and demotic script—a later, faster form of hieroglyphs. In 1801 Great Britain took control of Egypt, and the Rosetta stone was sent to the British Museum in London. Historians hoped that the inscription would help cryptographers (people who figure out how to read codes) decipher hieroglyphs. Their efforts were in vain.

*The first section of the **Rosetta stone** is in hieroglyphs, the central section is in Egyptian demotic, and the last section is in Greek. The broken-off edges were searched for, but they were never found.*

THE ROSETTA STONE

The Rosetta stone is the key that unlocked the secrets of ancient Egyptian hieroglyphs. For Jean-François Champollion, the interpretation of the picture symbols fulfilled a lifelong ambition. He had been obsessed with hieroglyphs since the age of ten and was determined to decipher them. His achievement opened up the entire written history of ancient Egypt.

People flocked to the British Museum in London, England, to see the Rosetta Stone.

A FORGOTTEN SCRIPT

Dating back over 5,000 years, hieroglyphs were used by the ancient Egyptians in state and ceremonial documents and on the walls of monuments and tombs. But the 700 picture symbols were too detailed to be used on a daily basis, and a faster form of writing evolved. This was called demotic script. Toward the end of the A.D. 300s hieroglyphs were banned by the Christian church because they were considered pagan. Soon there was no one left who could understand them, and the script was forgotten until Champollion translated it around 1,400 years later.

*These **hieroglyphs** are from the tomb of Horemheb, a king of Egypt (ruled 1348–1320 B.C.). The two ovals are cartouches containing hieroglyphs that make up a royal name. It was by looking at cartouches like these that Champollion deciphered hieroglyphs.*

DECIPHERING THE STONE

Twenty years later a French linguist, Jean-François Champollion (1790–1832), began working on the stone. Champollion had a good knowledge of ancient languages. Using Greek and Coptic, a language descended from ancient Egyptian, Champollion was able to identify the hieroglyphic characters of the name Ptolomys (Ptolemy). They were inscribed inside an oval called a cartouche, used for the names of rulers. Champollion then used the letters P, L, and O to unravel another cartouche—this time for Kliopadra (Cleopatra). Although there was still much work to do, Champollion had cracked the code!

"The most important event of the second millennium"

GRAHAM GREEN
Chairman of the Trustees of the British Museum, London, England, 1996–2002

Ancient tomb of a young king

In the desert to the west of Egypt's Nile river lies the Valley of the Kings. Around 3,000 years ago the rulers of Egypt, called pharaohs, chose to be buried there. By the early 1900s (A.D.) around 60 of their tombs had been discovered, but the treasures that had once surrounded the dead kings had disappeared long before. In 1922 the British archaeologist Howard Carter (1874–1939) uncovered the perfectly preserved tomb of an Egyptian pharaoh. It belonged to the young king Tutankhamen (ruled c. 1333–1324 B.C.).

THE ARCHAEOLOGIST

Howard Carter visited Egypt several times from the age of 17, making copies of tomb paintings and inscriptions for Egyptian archaeologists. He started his own excavations and was convinced that Tutankhamen's tomb was buried in the Valley of the Kings. In 1914 he began an excavation sponsored by Lord Caernarvon (1866–1923), a wealthy British aristocrat.

THE HIDDEN STEPS

For years Carter had no luck, but on November 4, 1922 his team uncovered stone steps leading to a sealed doorway. Carter saw that the seals were inscribed with the name Nebkheprure, one of the names used by Tutankhamen. Astonishing! Could this be the long-lost tomb? Carter sent a telegram to Lord Caernarvon and waited for him to arrive in Egypt.

"At last have made wonderful discovery."

HOWARD CARTER (*writing in a telegram*)
Archaeologist

This was the sight that met Carter's eyes when he first peered inside of the tomb.

THE EXCAVATION

The excavation of Tutankhamen's tomb took Carter ten long years. He worked painstakingly—numbering, drawing, photographing, and measuring every object in the tomb's four rooms. Larger items had to be broken apart, and protection from the dry desert air was a major concern. The treasures were taken to Cairo, Egypt, and put on display. Later, in the 1960s and 1970s, they were exhibited around the world. Today the treasures are back in Cairo, and Tutankhamen's mummified remains have returned to the Valley of the Kings.

THE GLIMMER OF GOLD

Nineteen days later Lord Caernarvon stood by Carter as he opened up the doorway. Behind it lay a passage leading to another door. Carter carved a hole in this doorway, lit a candle, and peered in. As he later wrote, he saw "strange animals, statues, and gold—everywhere the glint of gold." Behind the door was a small chamber filled with furniture, chariots, weapons, jewelry—everything the pharaoh would need in the afterlife. It was an Egyptian treasure trove.

Burial goods *found inside the tomb include this gold ornamental dagger and scabbard (left) and a gold collar (right) decorated with Horus, the hawk-headed god of the sky.*

TUTANKHAMEN'S TOMB

Carter was about to give up the search for Tutankhamen's tomb when the steps were found. The discovery was greater than any of his dreams—it was the first tomb of an Egyptian pharaoh to be found perfectly preserved, inspiring a huge interest in Egyptology.

Tutankhamen's mummy was found inside of this **coffin case** *made out of solid gold. The two tiny mummies of his stillborn children were also found close by.*

Ancient scrolls in a desert cave

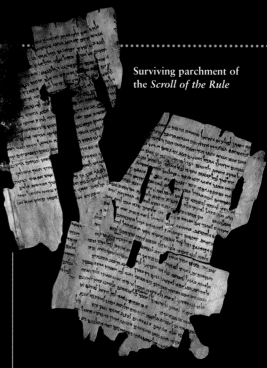

Surviving parchment of the *Scroll of the Rule*

In January 1947 a young Bedouin, Muhammed Adh-Dhib, was herding his goats in Qumran, Israel, on the northwest shore of the Dead Sea. It was evening, and realizing that one of his goats was missing, Adh-Dhib started to search for it among the rocks. By chance, he threw a stone into a cave and heard some pottery breaking. He decided to return the next day to find out what it was. Adh-Dhib was about to make a sensational find.

These pieces of parchment, known as the **Scroll of the Rule**, *have been pieced together by scholars. The text outlines the rules of the Essenes' religious life and the punishments for those who broke them.*

JARS IN A CAVE

When Muhammed Adh-Dhib searched the cave in Qumran, he found seven old pottery jars. He lifted the lids, looked inside, and pulled out some ancient scrolls wrapped in linen. Adh-Dhib took the scrolls and sold them to an antiques dealer in Bethlehem. Three of the scrolls were bought by an archaeologist; the other four made their way to the U.S. They returned to Israel eight years later. Meanwhile scholars around the world heard about the scrolls and flocked to Jerusalem to study them.

The Dead Sea scrolls are displayed in a specially built museum called the **Shrine of the Book.** *The dome-shaped building is partly underground in order to represent the cave where the scrolls were found. The scrolls are on display for only six months at a time. Experts are trying to protect them from humidity, temperature changes, and pollution.*

INSIGHT INTO JEWISH LIFE

The Dead Sea scrolls are a collection of Jewish documents written in Hebrew and Aramaic, the everyday language in the region 2,000 years ago. Some are copies of books in the Bible; some are commentaries on the Bible texts; others describe the beliefs, rituals, and political life of Jews at that time.

ANCIENT BIBLE TEXTS

The scrolls were extremely fragile. No wonder—they were 2,000 years old. Scholars studied them carefully. They eventually figured out that they were sections of an ancient copy of the Old Testament—1,000 years older than any known Hebrew Bible. There was huge excitement. More searches were carried out in the caves around Qumran, and thousands more pieces of parchment were found. Scholars have spent years piecing them together and interpreting the ancient texts.

HIDDEN FROM THE ROMANS

No one knows the exact truth about the Dead Sea scrolls, but most scholars believe that they were written by a Jewish people called the Essenes, who lived in Qumran around 2,000 years ago. Expecting an attack by their Roman rulers, they might have placed their scrolls in pottery jars and then hidden these inside the caves. Two hundred years later the texts are on display in Jerusalem in a museum known as the Shrine of the Book. Possibly, as scholars continue to study them, we will learn more about the Essenes and their ancient texts.

DEAD SEA SCROLLS

The story of the discovery of the scrolls captured the world's imagination. The texts themselves provide an insight into Jewish life and culture from around 200 B.C. to A.D. 70. They offer glimpses of the turbulent times leading up to and during the lifetime of Jesus. As a result, they are of huge interest to both Jewish and Christian scholars.

*These **pottery jars** are similar to those that held the Dead Sea scrolls. The scrolls were found in a cave overlooking the Dead Sea.*

An ancient city built in rock

In 1812 a young Swiss traveler named Johann Burckhardt (1784–1817) was traveling in southern Jordan when he heard about a wonderful ruined city hidden in the desert. He believed that it was Petra, an ancient Arab trading center that had fallen into ruin long ago. Burckhardt longed to find Petra, but how?

"A rose-red city— half as old as time!"

JOHN WILLIAM BURGON
Biblical scholar (1819–1888)

*The Nabataeans carved hundreds of **tombs** into the hillsides around Petra. The tombs displayed a family's wealth and honored those who were buried inside.*

PETRA
When Burckhardt discovered Petra, he told the world about a city deep inside a desert gorge. Since then travelers and historians have visited Petra and learned more about the Nabataeans and their world. Today Petra is a protected site and Jordan's best-known tourist attraction.

WHAT WAS PETRA?
Around 2,000 years ago Petra was the capital city of an Arab people known as the Nabataeans. It was a stopping place for the traders who crisscrossed the ancient world. Over hundreds of years the trade routes changed, and Petra was abandoned.

THE RUINS OF PETRA
Petra's ruined buildings are a spectacular sight in their rugged desert setting. Banquet halls, baths, tombs, and shrines were chiseled into the cliffs by local craftsmen. Many of the buildings were elaborately carved out, plastered, and brightly painted. As well as being skilled builders, the Nabataeans were clever engineers. Using three local springs, they designed an ingenious system of pipelines, tanks, and reservoirs that supplied the city's inhabitants with water for their crops, livestock, gardens, and fountains and also for their homes and public buildings.

The towering facade of El Deir, the Monastery, has been carved out of solid rock.

The first building that Burckhardt would have seen when he entered Petra is El Khazneh, the Treasury. This ornate, pillared building is more than 148 ft. (45m) tall. It was carved out by men who were clearly as skilled at climbing as they were at carving! The building is known as the Treasury because of the urn at the top, which is believed to hold great riches.

BURCKHARDT'S PLAN

By 1812 Petra had not appeared on a map of the region for more than 1,000 years. Burckhardt knew that if he was going to find the city, he would need a local guide. But the region was dangerous for visitors, and he was afraid of being arrested as a spy. So he came up with a clever plan. He disguised himself as a Muslim pilgrim by growing a beard and wearing Arab clothing. He told people that he wanted to make a sacrifice to the prophet Aaron (c. 15th–13th century B.C.), who was said to be buried in a tomb close to Petra. The plan worked—in a few days Burckhardt had his guide, and he was on his way.

A DAZZLING SIGHT

After traveling through the desert for days Burckhardt's guide turned off of the path and entered a narrow ravine. They continued on between its towering walls until suddenly a spectacular building came into view. There it was! They had arrived in Petra. Burckhardt was dazzled by the ancient city with its elaborate buildings carved into solid sandstone cliffs. He later told the world about his find. But it was two Frenchmen, Linant Bellefonds (1799–1883) and Leon de Laborde (1807–1869), who really put Petra on the map. In 1828 they spent one week sketching the city and published a volume of drawings. People were amazed, and since then travelers from all over the world have visited the site.

A Hindu temple in the jungle

Between A.D. 800–1300 a Hindu people called the Khmer ruled over most of Southeast Asia. Their capital city, Angkor, contained the greatest Hindu temple ever built. When the Khmer empire collapsed, Angkor and its temple were abandoned in the jungle and forgotten about for hundreds of years—until 1861.

"Grander than anything left to us by Greece or Rome"

HENRI MAHOUT
Botanist and explorer

Angkor Wat, *the largest religious monument in the world, looms out of the forest. Its five carved towers represent the peaks of Mount Meru, the mythological home of the gods and center of the Hindu universe.*

ANGKOR WAT
Mahout's discovery of Angkor Wat brought an architectural masterpiece to the world's attention. The ruined city is a rich resource for historians, providing a unique insight into the Khmer empire and the everyday life of the Khmer.

THE BOTANIST
French botanist Henri Mahout was exploring a remote area of northern Cambodia when he heard tales about a lost city in the jungle. Intrigued, he persuaded a local missionary to lead him to the mystical place. Traveling first by canoe and then on foot, they finally reached some ancient ruins. Grand gateways, carved walls, and ornate terraces were overgrown with trees and vines. Incredible! Mahout had discovered Angkor and its long-lost temple.

WHAT WAS ANGKOR?
Mahout did not realize the full size and magnificence of what he had found. At its peak, Angkor, which means "the city," covered a huge area with an intricate network of roads, causeways, and irrigation canals. Huge staircases led up to a series of terraces, where vast temples and palaces rose up toward the sky. The greatest of these temples was Angkor Wat.

*For 600 years the enormous temple of **Angkor Wat** lay hidden in the jungle of northern Cambodia. When it was discovered, archaeologists stripped the forest from the temple ruins, uncovering porches and walkways with carved balustrades. Paths were cleared away around the ancient complex, and a road was built from the nearby town of Siem Reap. Years of restoration work still remain.*

The face of Avalokiteshvara, a Buddhist deity, carved in the wall

INTRICATE STONE CARVINGS

The temple of Angkor Wat was built in the 1100s in honor of the Hindu god Vishnu. But it was ransacked in 1177, and part of it had to be rebuilt. This time it was dedicated to the Buddha. It is surrounded by 2.5 mi. (4km) of walls that are covered in carvings from Hindu and Buddhist mythology. Other carvings depict the Khmer working, hunting, taking care of their animals, or riding elephants into battle.

ANGKOR WAT RESTORED

When he returned to France, Mahout told the authorities about his discovery. At that time Cambodia was a French colony, and the government sent teams of archaeologists and scholars to begin restoring the site. Cambodians and visitors from around the world began visiting Angkor to marvel at the ruins. Sadly Angkor Wat was "lost" again in the early 1970s during a bitter civil war. But today the site has reopened, and the visitors have returned.

Precious cargo under the sea

I n the mid-1980s a Vietnamese fisherman was out in the South China Sea. He was amazed when, instead of the usual red snappers, he caught something else on his hook. It was a concrete-covered lump of iron containing several pieces of blue and white porcelain. The china looked old, and the fisherman thought it might be valuable. He had no idea what it was doing in the sea.

A GOOD CATCH

The man was fishing 100 mi. (160km) off the coast of south Vietnam, near the province of Vung Tau. He had always had good luck there, but his latest catch was the best so far. The fisherman went back to the area several times. He pulled up countless pieces of porcelain and sold them to antiques dealers for high prices. Eventually the Vietnamese authorities heard about the porcelain and decided to investigate. A salvage company began work in 1990. Incredible! Divers found an old Chinese trading ship, known as a lorcha, lying on the seabed. Thousands of pieces of porcelain lay in and around the remains of the hull.

The Vietnamese fisherman pulled up only a small part of the cargo. Divers found thousands of **pieces of porcelain** *coated in sand and shells. The wreck was an old Chinese trading ship around 112 ft. (34m) long and 33 ft. (10m) wide. It lay in 115 ft. (35m) of water.*

FAMOUS PORCELAIN

The porcelain found on the Vung Tau shipwreck was made around the time of the Chinese emperor Kan Xi (1662–1722), the third emperor of the Ching dynasty. It was made out of the most delicate clay, and the elegant pieces, with their blue and white designs, were very popular amongst wealthy Europeans in the 1600s. The craze for Chinese goods, called "China mania," led to a highly profitable trade. Teapots, goblets, and other pieces were specifically designed by Chinese craftsmen for the European market.

Some of the porcelain from the Vung Tau shipwreck

THE SHIPWRECK

Coins found at the site helped the divers date the ship back to around 1690. The wooden planks were charred, suggesting the ship sank as the result of a fire—possibly started by pirates, lightning, or an accident. The lorcha, like many other ships at the time, was probably traveling there from China to the island of Java. There the cargo, bound for the Netherlands, would have been transferred to another ship. Instead it sank with the lorcha to the ocean floor.

THE CARGO

The divers came across a wide assortment of goods that had been part of the lorcha's cargo—including dishes, bamboo combs, inkwells, tweezers, and dice. But the most precious pieces of cargo were the porcelain items, many of them miraculously found in one piece. Around 48,000 pieces were recovered. Out of these, thousands went to museums in Vietnam, and 28,000 pieces were taken to Amsterdam in the Netherlands, where they were auctioned in 1992. They sold for $7.3 million!

VUNG TAU SHIPWRECK

The discovery of the shipwreck and its precious cargo was an exciting find for historians. It provided information not only about a 300-year-old cargo ship but also about Chinese porcelain and the trading links that existed at that time between China and Europe. Visitors to museums in Vietnam are able to view the beautiful porcelain and learn about its fascinating story.

Silent warriors guard a tomb

In 1974 a group of farmers were digging a well near the city of Xi'an in northern China when they stumbled across something surprising. Buried in the ground were several carved heads made out of pottery. The men took the statues home and informed the authorities. Soon an archaeologist arrived in Xi'an to study and learn more about the statues. He set up a tent in the middle of the field and began digging. It was not long before he made a sensational discovery.

THE IMPERIAL BURIAL SITE

When archaeologist Yuan Zhongyi was sent to a field in northern China to investigate some buried figurines, he thought he would be there for around one week. But after digging in the ground for a few days his team uncovered something. Extraordinary! It was a gigantic pit covering almost 3.5 acres (14,300m²). It had a wooden roof made out of pine logs and a floor paved with brick, and it contained row upon row of life-size statues. They were an army of warriors beautifully crafted out of baked clay known as terra-cotta. Yuan Zhongyi soon realized that this must be part of the burial site of Emperor Qin Shi Huangdi (259–210 B.C.). He was the first emperor of China and was buried in a tomb in the area.

A terra-cotta warrior *silently stands guard by the emperor's tomb. In early civilizations servants were often sentenced to death to serve their ruler in the afterlife. Rather than sacrifice an entire army, Emperor Qin was buried with a symbolic army of life-size, terra-cotta soldiers.*

Qin Shi Huangdi, first emperor of China and founder of the Qin Dynasty

TERRA-COTTA ARMY

The discovery of the terra-cotta warriors has brought a unique work of art to the world's attention. The intricate detail of the figurines provides historians with a rich source of information about the early years of the Chinese Empire, and the discovery of his army has provided Emperor Qin Shi Huangdi with the glory and immortality he desired.

*Originally painted in bright colors, this **terra-cotta archer** has faded and lost his wooden crossbow. Other members of the army include officers, cavalrymen, and charioteers with chariots and mighty horses. Tall, well proportioned, and physically alert, the warriors look like they are ready for battle. Their faces are intelligent, resourceful, and sincere. This is an emperor's ideal army—one that would defend him to the death!*

THE EMPEROR

Emperor Qin Shi Huangdi was a major figure in Chinese history—a leader, conqueror, and ruthless tyrant. He successfully united six warring states into the land of modern-day China. As soon as he became emperor, Qin ordered 700,000 slave laborers to begin working on the tomb in which he would one day be buried, and he commanded craftsmen to make a terra-cotta army to protect him in the afterlife.

THE EXCAVATION

Archaeologists continued digging at the site. In 1976 they found a second pit and then two more pits. One of the pits was empty, but the others contained almost 8,000 statues. The archaeologists faced a huge task, and in order to protect the fragile figurines, they temporarily refilled the new pits. Since then two of the pits have been excavated. The figurines have been displayed in Qin Shi Huangdi's museum, which was built near the site. It is now one of the greatest tourist attractions in the world.

Part of the Terra-Cotta Army

MAKING THE WARRIORS

Each warrior in the Terra-Cotta Army is a unique individual and can be distinguished from all of the others. Their heads were made from one of around 12 different molds, and the eyes and noses were sculpted by hand. Beards, mustaches, hairstyles, and headgear helped create an individual appearance, while arms, legs, and armor added additional variety. After being fired the figurines were painted and given bronze swords and wooden scabbards (cases), crossbows, and spears.

Hoaxes and frauds

The world of discoveries is always open to questions because some finds are not what they appear to be. How do you distinguish the genuine from the fake and the insignificant from an authentic gem? After proudly announcing a major new discovery some experts have faced embarrassment when the discovery that caused such excitement was exposed as a fake. Other experts have missed valuable genuine artifacts right under their noses. The true identity of a new discovery is easy to mistake, and even some of the world's most respected scientists and institutions have been fooled by the ingenuity and daredevil approach of these impressive fakes.

Famous portrait of a president

F rom time to time the art world makes interesting and profitable discoveries. Long-lost pictures by famous artists suddenly turn up in dusty attics and forgotten cupboards or are found hanging unrecognized in antique stores or auction rooms. In 1989 a British art dealer was in New York City looking for some interesting paintings. Suddenly, across an auction room, a familiar portrait caught his eye.

THE AUCTION ROOM

Gavin Graham was visiting the U.S., looking for new pictures for his gallery in London, England. There was an auction of American art coming up by a dealer in New York City, and Graham went along to see what was for sale. He was not expecting to find a bargain. He assumed American dealers would bid for work by good American artists, which would raise the price.

This portrait of George Washington is known as the **Gibbs-Channing-Avery portrait.** *It is one of 18 similar works by Gilbert Stuart known as the Vaughan group. It is a copy of an original portrait by Stuart, painted in 1795.*

A portrait of George Washington is reproduced on the one dollar bill. It is based on one of Gilbert Stuart's portraits, painted in around 1796.

PAINTING WASHINGTON'S PORTRAIT

The rediscovered portrait of George Washington was one of Stuart's copies of a portrait he painted during a live sitting. This took place at the end of Washington's second term as president, when his political career was ending and only three years before his death. Stuart asked Washington to sit for him so that he could paint his face more accurately. He used a model when he painted the body. Washington disliked sitting for portraits, but he did it out of a sense of duty. He looks like a typical 18th-century gentleman in a black velvet suit. His white hair is powdered and tied back in the style of the time.

THE PORTRAIT

Around 200 pictures were to be auctioned, but only one caught Graham's eye. It was a painting of George Washington (1732–1799), the first U.S. president. Art experts know that the official portraits of Washington were painted by Gilbert Stuart (1755–1828). Stuart copied most of these from his original portraits. Lesser known, less talented artists had also painted thousands of copies of the portraits, and the painting that Graham saw for sale was described as one of these. But Graham was not so sure. Looking at it carefully, he judged that it had real quality, and at the auction the next day he bought it for around $3,000.

THE DISCOVERY

Back in London, Graham sent his picture to an art expert for a thorough investigation. Remarkable! The painting was one of Gilbert Stuart's portraits of Washington, painted in 1796. It had been commissioned by James Madison (1751–1836), the fourth president of the U.S., and was later given to his private secretary. The painting had been passed down through the family but in recent years had been "lost." Graham, of course, was delighted with the news. Now that its true identity was revealed, the painting was worth more. It was sold to an American gallery for around $375,000.

PORTRAIT OF GEORGE WASHINGTON

The discovery of one of Gilbert Stuart's portraits was a success story for Graham. Described in an auction room catalogue as an unremarkable copy, the portrait made Graham a big profit. One of the U.S.'s most famous paintings is now correctly identified, well cared for, and returned to its country of origin.

Discovery of an ancient skull

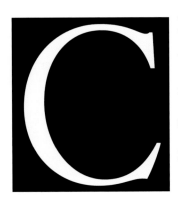

Charles Dawson (1864–1916) was a lawyer and amateur archaeologist. In 1912 he found some fossilized human remains in a gravel pit in Piltdown in Sussex, England. The discovery was greeted with great excitement. Some experts believed the fossils belonged to a new species— a "missing link" between apes and humans.

WHAT DID IT MEAN?

Woodward believed that the human skull bones and the apelike jaw belonged to a prehistoric human being, which he called *Eoanthropus dawsoni*. Some scientists thought the bones belonged to different species of animals. But Woodward argued that they must belong to one species because they looked so similar in color and age and were found so close together. Also the flat teeth were typical of humans, not apes, which suggested that they belonged with the human skull bone. This was undeniably true, and Woodward's views ruled the day.

THE "DISCOVERY"

The fragments that Dawson found in the pit in Piltdown included skull bones, teeth, and flint tools. He took them to Arthur Smith Woodward (1864–1944) at London's Natural History Museum. Woodward was so interested in them that he joined the excavation in Piltdown. Soon more ancient animal remains were found. The most significant of these was a fragment of an apelike jawbone with two flat, molar teeth.

PILTDOWN MAN
Piltdown Man was one of the longest-running frauds. At the time the ancient skull bones and jawbone were believed to be the oldest human remains ever found anywhere in the world. The case wasted years of scientists' time. However, it taught them to be skeptical and to investigate data carefully.

Dawson *(left)* and Woodward *(right)* sieve material at the gravel pit in Piltdown.

The apelike jawbone of Piltdown Man containing two flat, humanlike teeth

For more than 40 years **Piltdown Man** *was accepted by many British scientists. The prehistoric human being* Eoanthropus dawsoni *appeared in textbooks and encyclopedias as the missing link between apes and humans.*

DOUBTS ARISE

Years passed, and as more prehistoric human remains were found around the world, Piltdown Man began to look "wrong." While it had a small brain case with an apelike jaw, the other finds had a larger brain case with a smaller, humanlike jaw. In 1953 a South African scientist named Joseph S.Weiner (1915–1982) claimed that Piltdown Man must be a fraud. Using the latest testing techniques, he and other scientists proved that the skull and jaw came from different species and were from different times. Piltdown Man was a hoax. Who was responsible? Dawson is a prime suspect, but no one actually knows.

A 1915 painting showing scientists examining the Piltdown skull

HOW PILTDOWN WAS EXPOSED

A new test called the fluorine dating method helped expose the Piltdown hoax. Buried bones absorb fluorine from the soil, and the amount increases over time. The fluorine content of the skull fragments revealed that the jawbone and teeth were modern. They had been stained to match the ancient skull. The jaw fragment was later proven to have come from an orangutan. Microscopic examination of the teeth revealed that they had been filed down to make them look human.

A reconstruction of
Eoanthropus dawsoni,
widely known as
Piltdown Man

Photographs of a fantasy world

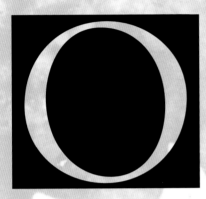

One evening in 1917 in Yorkshire, England, 16-year-old Elsie Wright (1901–1988) and her 9-year-old cousin Frances Griffiths (1907–1986) came home late for dinner. The two girls were scolded, but they had an extraordinary excuse. They told their parents that they had been watching fairies. Elsie later produced photographs to support their story, but were they genuine? Were the girls telling the truth?

FAIRY PHOTOS

Elsie Wright and Frances Griffiths spent many hours playing near Cottingley Beck, a stream in the village of Cottingley in Yorkshire, England. This infuriated Frances' mother. When Frances explained that she and Elsie had seen fairies, her mother became angry. Then Elsie produced photographs. Unbelievable! Frances was surrounded by tiny winged people.

THE SENSATION

Elsie's mother was interested in spiritualism (the belief in spirits and the supernatural). She sent the photos to Edward Gardner (d. 1970), a well-known spiritualist, who sent them to a photographic expert. He also contacted fellow spiritualist Arthur Conan Doyle (1859–1930), author of the Sherlock Holmes novels. They all believed the photos were real, so Conan Doyle published them in a magazine—which caused a sensation!

HOW DID THEY DO IT?

The girls' hoax was inspired by one of Frances' favorite books, *Princess Mary's Gift Book*. In 1917, when her parents moved from South Africa to England, she brought her copy with her. That day in Yorkshire when Frances was scolded so severely by her mother, Elsie wanted to cheer up her cousin. Being a talented artist, the older girl suggested that they copy fairy drawings out of Frances' book. They copied the figures onto construction paper and then carefully cut them out. They took the fairies to the stream and pinned them onto the mossy branches of bushes and trees. In some of the photographs the top of the pin is clearly visible! Then they took several photographs of themselves with the fairies in different positions and developed them in Elsie's father's darkroom. Little did the two young girls realize that their innocent childhood game would cause such a shock and would puzzle the world for 60 years.

Elsie Wright cutting out a paper fairy to demonstrate how she and her cousin faked the photographs of the Cottingley fairies 60 years earlier

The famous photographs *show Elsie Wright (left) and Frances Griffiths (above) with fairies in Yorkshire, England.*

"I have seen the very interesting photos . . . they are amazing."

ARTHUR CONAN DOYLE
Author and spiritualist

THE CONFESSION

Millions of people believed that the fairies were real. Many others thought the photos were fake, but whenever the girls were questioned they always stuck to their story. Years passed, and slowly the commotion died down. The girls both got married and spent many years overseas. It was not until the early 1980s, long after Gardner and Conan Doyle had died, that the truth emerged. Elsie, by then an old woman, confessed that the fairies were fakes. The girls' story had been a silly prank that had escalated out of control. Fakes or not, the photos never lost their fame. In 1998, after Elsie and Frances had died, they were sold for more than $35,000!

THE COTTINGLEY FAIRIES

The photos of the Cottingley fairies, believed by some at the time to prove that fairies did exist, were some of the most talked-about pictures of the 1900s. It is truly incredible that with nothing more than a camera and an ability to tell tall tales, two young girls managed to pull off such an extraordinary hoax. Many years later they admitted that they had been amazed that people were fooled by the paper cutouts.

New painting by a master

In 1937 a Dutch art historian, Abraham Bredius (1855–1946), was asked to examine a recently discovered painting. Bredius was an expert on the Dutch artist Jan Vermeer (1632–1675). When Bredius saw the painting, he was amazed. It was an unknown, genuine work by Vermeer!

Genuine paintings by Vermeer, such as **The Lacemaker** *(above), mainly showed domestic scenes.*

Van Meegeren working on the "Vermeer" that cleared him at his trial

HOW DID HE DO IT?
Van Meegeren's paintings were technically perfect. He bought and cleaned works of art from the 1600s, leaving a network of cracks in the bottom layer of paint. He used pigments that matched what was available in Vermeer's lifetime and mixed them with synthetic resin instead of oil so that the paint hardened and looked very old. He then "aged" his paintings by baking them.

THE DISCOVERY
As Bredius studied the newly discovered painting, called *Christ and the Disciples at Emmaus*, he was overjoyed. He had always believed that since Vermeer had visited Italy he must have been influenced by Italian artists and produced religious paintings, as well as paintings of domestic scenes for which he was famous. This new painting, a religious subject in the Italian style, proved Bredius right. A museum in Rotterdam in the Netherlands bought the painting with the help of several huge donations.

A SHOCK ARREST
At this time many countries in Europe were at war with Germany, and the Netherlands was occupied by the German army. In 1945, as the war was ending, another Vermeer turned up in the collection of a German commander, Hermann Goering (1893–1946). Papers proved that Goering had bought the painting from Dutch artist Hans van Meegeren (1889–1947). Van Meegeren was arrested for collaborating with the enemy—an offense punishable by death.

THE UNKNOWN VERMEER

The Van Meegeren case rocked the art world and forced it to change its ways. "Experts" were no longer considered to be the most reliable way of evaluating a painting. High-tech tests, such as X-rays and electron microscopy, are now used to identify fakes.

Van Meegeren's painting, entitled **Christ and the Disciples at Emmaus**, *was painted in Vermeer's early style and based on a similar painting, which Vermeer would have seen, by the Italian artist Caravaggio (1573–1610). It fooled art experts until Van Meegeren was forced to confess.*

THE COURT CASE

At his trial in 1947 Van Meegeren came up with a sensational defense—he had not collaborated with the enemy; he had painted the unknown "Vermeer" himself! Not only that, but he had also forged the painting of *Christ and the Disciples at Emmaus.* Art historians could hardly believe their ears. To prove his case, Van Meegeren painted another "Vermeer" while he was in custody. He was charged with forgery and given one year in jail. One month later, having embarrassed the art world, he suddenly got sick and died.

> "I determined to prove my worth as a painter by making a perfect 17th-century canvas."
>
> **HANS VAN MEEGEREN**
> *Artist*

German leader's long-lost diaries

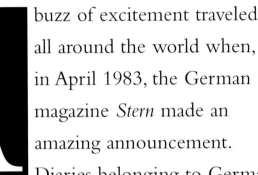

A buzz of excitement traveled all around the world when, in April 1983, the German magazine *Stern* made an amazing announcement. Diaries belonging to German dictator Adolf Hitler (1889–1945) had been found, and extracts would soon be published in the magazine.

THE DISCOVERY

Hitler's newly discovered diaries contained 62 handwritten volumes with entries from the years 1932–1945, both before and during World War II. They had supposedly been flown out of Berlin, Germany, before Hitler's death, but the plane had crashed. The diaries somehow made their way into the hands of *Stern* reporter Gerd Heidemann (b. 1931), who bought the exclusive publishing rights for around $5 million.

Adolf Hitler *was an infamous historical figure. Stern hoped that his diaries would reveal his innermost thoughts and feelings.*

THE HITLER DIARIES

The Hitler diaries were the most expensive fraud in publishing history. Stern magazine journalists were so desperate to guard the "scoop" that they failed to carry out basic checks. They desperately wanted the diaries to be real, and along with several historians, they were fooled.

*Controversial historian **David Irving** (b. 1938) declared that the Hitler diaries were fake at a Stern press conference on April 25, 1983. He had originally said they were authentic.*

THE WORLD'S REACTION

Knowing the diaries would attract thousands of readers, many journals rushed to buy the story. U.S. magazine *Newsweek* and British newspapers *The Times* and *The Sunday Times* offered *Stern* a fortune for the right to publish translated extracts. Astonishing! The diaries were declared to be authentic, first by leading historian Hugh Trevor-Roper (1914–2003) and then by handwriting experts, who compared the pages with other Hitler writing. They agreed they were written by the same hand.

THE FORGERY EXPOSED

The story suddenly stopped dead in its tracks. Forensic tests proved that the diaries were forgeries after all. The person who had sold them to *Stern* turned out to be Konrad Kujau (1938–2000), a dealer and forger of Nazi memorabilia who had learned to imitate Hitler's handwriting perfectly. Kujau was working together with Heidemann, who had skimmed off most of *Stern*'s money for himself. The two men were arrested, convicted of fraud, and sentenced to four-and-a-half years in prison.

A FORGERY REVEALED

Forensic tests carried out on the diaries proved that they had been written long after World War II. Under ultraviolet lights, the paper showed a whitening agent that was used only after 1954. Chromatography—a process used to separate dyes—chemically proved that the ink was modern. An additional test that measured the evaporation of chloride from the ink proved that the writing was less than one year old. The diaries even contained historical inaccuracies. They were fakes!

Heidemann (right) facing reporters after the hoax was exposed

Landmark fossil found in China

In 1999 the owner of a dinosaur museum in the U.S. saw an interesting specimen at a fossil fair. He thought the fossil was so exciting that he paid around $75,000 for it. It was a feathered creature that seemed to be half bird, half dinosaur. Could it be the "missing link" that proved that birds evolved from dinosaurs?

NEW EVIDENCE

The fossil had a head and arms like those of a bird but the tail, legs, and feet of a dinosaur. It seemed to be the evidence that scientists had been hoping to find for 130 years—a species that would prove Huxley's theory that birds evolved from dinosaurs (see page 13). News of the find reached the National Geographic Society. They wanted to be the first to tell the story.

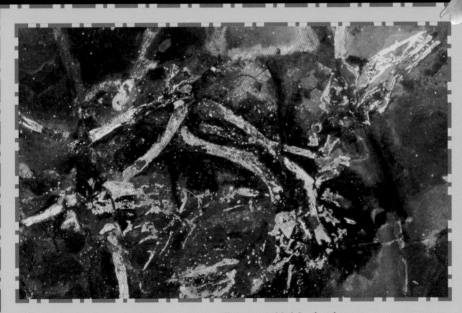

The *Archaeoraptor* fossil, "found" in a 125-million-year-old slab of rock

FOSSIL FAKES

The Liaoning province of China has produced many exciting fossils, but it also produces fakes. Workers are paid to dig underground, and they earn a bonus if they find a complete fossil. The farmer who found and made the *Archaeoraptor* fossil knew he would get more money if he had a complete specimen. No one knows if he deliberately made a fake or if he thought he was glueing together pieces of the same creature to make a whole one.

"I am 100 percent sure . . . we have to admit that *Archaeoraptor* is a faked specimen."

XU XING
Paleontologist

THE SPECIES IS NAMED

Scientists began to investigate. They had little information about the fossil because it had been illegally exported from Liaoning in China. With some doubt, they confirmed that it was a birdlike creature from the pelvis up and a dinosaur from the pelvis down. They named the new species *Archaeoraptor liaoningensis*. They were still discussing the fossil when *National Geographic* magazine published pictures of the find.

This reconstruction of the "new species" **Archaeoraptor liaoningensis** *was displayed in the National Geographic Society offices in Washington, D.C. It was viewed by thousands of visitors.*

! ARCHAEORAPTOR LIAONINGENSIS

The fossil fake was a humiliation for National Geographic. If they had waited for a full investigation, they would have discovered the truth about the fossil. However, the two parts of the false fossil were both later identified as important new species in their own right.

EXPOSED

Then, in Liaoning province, a Chinese paleontologist, Xu Xing, discovered the counterslab of the fossil—the other half of the rock in which the fossil was found, which showed its mirror image. The tail in the counterslab was the same, but the rest of the body was different. The fossil in the U.S. was a fake—the tail had been glued to another fossil. Xu Xing sent a telegram to *National Geographic* to tell them the bad news.

Index

Acknowledgments

The publisher would like to thank the following for permission to reproduce their material. Every care has been taken to trace copyright holders. However, if there have been unintentional omissions or failure to trace copyright holders, we apologize and will, if informed, endeavor to make corrections in any future edition.

Key: *b* = bottom, *c* = center, *l* = left, *r* = right, *t* = top

Cover Archivo Iconografico, S.A./CORBIS; 1 Mary Evans Picture Library; 2–3 National Geographic Image Collection/Kenneth Garrett; 4–5 Bettman/Corbis; 6 Dr Robert Ballard; 8–9 Natural History Museum, London; 10*tr* Natural History Museum, London; 10–11 Warren Photographic; 11*cr* Natural History Museum, London; 12*bl* Natural History Museum, London; 13 Warren Photographic; 14 Chris Lisle/Corbis; 15*tr* & 15*c* SPL/Silkeborg Museum, Denmark, Munoz-Yague; 16 Corbis; 18*l* SPL/Sinclair Stammers; 19*tl* & 19*tr* South African Institute for Aquatic Biodiversity courtesy of SAIAB; 19*b* SPL/Peter Scoones; 20*bl* Francis G. Mayer/Corbis; 20*c* Bettman/Corbis; 21*bl* The Image Bank © Getty Images; 21*r* Terry Whittaker, Frank Lane Picture Agency/Corbis; 22 Bool Dan/Corbis Sygma; 23*tl* Advertising Archive/RKO; 23*r* Gavriel/Corbis; 24–25 Christie's Images/Corbis; 26 Bettman/Corbis; 27*tr* HIP/The British Museum; 27*cr* Polak Matthew/Corbis Sygma; 27 *bc* Lowell Georgia/Corbis; 28*c* Bat Conservation International courtesy of © Merlin D. Tuttle; 28*bl* Lowell Georgia/Corbis; 30*bl* & 30*tr* Galaxy Pictures/NOAA; 31*b* Galaxy Pictures/NOAA; 31*cr* Ralph White/Corbis; 32*l* Bettman/Corbis; 33*tl* Bettman/Corbis; 33*b* David Batterbury, Eye Ubiquitous/Corbis; 34*bl* Hulton Getty; 35*t* Bettman/Corbis; 35*cr* Getty Images/Taxi; 36*b* Nik Wheeler/Corbis; 37*tc* Art Archive/Orleans House Gallery; 37*cl* Bettman/Corbis; 37*bl* Corbis; 38*tl* Natural History Museum, London; 38*b* Dave G. Houser/Corbis; 39 Art Archive/Bibliothéque des Arts Décoratifs Paris/Dagli Orti; 40*bl* Getty Images/Stone; 41*c* Leonard de Selva/Corbis; 41*tr* Art Archive/Muse Cernuschi Paris/Dagli Orti; 42–43 Historical Picture Archive/Corbis; 44*cl* National Geographic Image Collection/Hiram Bingham; 45*cl* Wolfgang Kaehler/Corbis; 45*r* Craig Lovell/Corbis; 46*bl* Leonard de Selva/Corbis; 46*tr* Ralph White/Corbis; 48*bl* Archivo Iconografico, S.A./Corbis; 49*t* & 49*br* Pierre Vauthey/Corbis Sygma; 50*b* HIP/The British Museum; 51*tr* Mary Evans Picture Library; 51*c* Gianni Dagli Orti/Corbis; 52*bl* Art Archive/Pharaonic Village, Cairo/Dagli Orti; 53*cl* Sandro Vannini/Corbis and Vanni Archive/Corbis; 53*r* National Geographic Image Collection/Kenneth Garrett; 54*bl* David Rubinger/Corbis; 54*tr* West Semitic Research/Dead Sea Scrolls Foundation/Corbis; 55*b* HIP/The British Museum; 55*r* Richard T. Nowitz/Corbis; 56*bl* Alison Wright/Corbis; 56*cr* Alan Towse, Ecoscene/Corbis; 57*c* Alison Wright/Corbis; 58*b* Kevin R. Morris/Corbis; 59*tl* Paul A. Souders/Corbis; 59*cr* Luca I. Tettoni/Corbis; 61*tc* Hallstrom Holdings courtesey of Michael Flecker; 62*l* Keren Su/Corbis; 63*tl* HIP/The British Museum; 63*cr* Asian Art and Archaeology, Inc./Corbis; 63*bc* Bridgeman Art Library; 64–65 Bettman/Corbis; 66*bl* Joseph Sohm, Visions of America/Corbis; 67*l* Francis G. Mayer/Corbis; 68*cr* & 68*br* Natural History Museum, London; 69*cr* Natural History Museum, London/The Geological Society; 70 Bettman/Corbis; 71 HIP/NMPFT; 72*bl* Bettman/Corbis; 72*tr* Francis G. Mayer/Corbis; 73 Museum Boijmans van Beuningen, Rotterdam; 74*c* Bettman/Corbis; 75*tl* Focal Point Publications courtesey of © David Irving; 75*br* Bettman/Corbis; 76*bl* & 77 National Geographic Image Collection/O. Louis Mazzatenta; 78–79 Natural History Museum, London; 80 Chris Lisle/Corbis.

The publisher would like to thank the following illustrators: Gino d'Achille 6; Jurgen Ziewe 16–17, 28–29, 46–47, 60–61, 68–69.